Sports Illustrated KIDS

THE KIDS' GUIDE TO SPORTS DESIGN AND ENGINEERING

BY THOMAS K. ADAMSON

CAPSTONE PRESS
a capstone imprint

SI Kids Guide Books are published by
Capstone Press
1710 Roe Crest Drive
North Mankato, Minnesota 56003
www.capstonepub.com

Library of Congress Cataloging-in-Publication Data
Adamson, Thomas K., 1970–
The kids' guide to sports design and engineering / by Thomas K.
Adamson.
    pages cm.—(Sports illustrated kids. SI kids guide books)
Includes index.
ISBN 978-1-4765-4155-6 (library binding)
ISBN 978-1-4765-5187-6 (paperback)
1. Sporting goods—Juvenile literature. 2. Industrial design—
Juvenile literature. 3. Human engineering—Juvenile literature.
4. Industrial engineering—Juvenile literature. I. Title.
GV745.A44 2014
688.7—dc23   2013032845

Editorial Credits
Anthony Wacholtz, editor; Sarah Bennett, designer; Eric Gohl,
media researcher; Charmaine Whitman, production specialist

Photo Credits
Alamy: Aurora Photos, 37, Phil Wigglesworth, 29; AP Photo:
PRNewsFoto/ANSYS, Inc., 45, Rajah Bose, 26 (top), Wade Payne, 25;
Corbis: Transtock/Robert Kerian, 4; Dreamstime: Piero Cruciatti,
cover; Getty Images: Hulton Archive, 23 (bottom); Newscom: Icon
SMI/David J. Griffin, 27, Icon SMI/DPP/Jean-Paul Thomas, 35, Icon
SMI/Ric Tapia, 15, Image Broker/Simone Brandt, 44, MCT/James
Borchuck, 22, Polli KRT, 7, Reuters/Shaun Best, 32, Staff KRT, 40,
VIEW View Pictures/Hufton + Crow, 34, ZUMA Press/Dan Krauss,
24; Science Source: Brian Bell, 18 (top), Ted Kinsman, 9 (bottom);
Shutterstock: Andresr, 8 (bottom), Papa Bravo, 42; Sports Illustrated:
Bill Frakes, 5, Bob Martin, 19, 20, Damian Strohmeyer, 14, David E.
Klutho, 6, 30–31, 41, Heinz Kluetmeier, 17, John Biever, 23 (top), John
W. McDonough, 18 (bottom), Robert Beck, 12, 13 (all), 16, 26 (bottom),
36, 39, Simon Bruty, 8 (top), 9 (top), 10, 11, 21, 28, 43; SuperStock:
Science Photo Library, 38; Wikipedia: Cacophony, 31 (bottom),
Laslovarga, 33

Design Elements: Shutterstock

Printed in the United States of America in Stevens Point, Wisconsin.
092013   007767WZS14

TABLE OF CONTENTS

ADVANCING THE GAME

Sports engineers might not be the superstars getting all the attention. But their work behind the scenes makes sports safer and more enjoyable. Engineers use technology to design better sports equipment. They help athletes avoid injury and improve their performance. Their innovations can also change how we watch sports. For example, many race cars use in-car cameras so fans can see what it's like to be inside a race car during an event. What if other sports could use cameras that way? What would the videos look like?

Cameras on race cars allow fans to see the race from the driver's point of view.

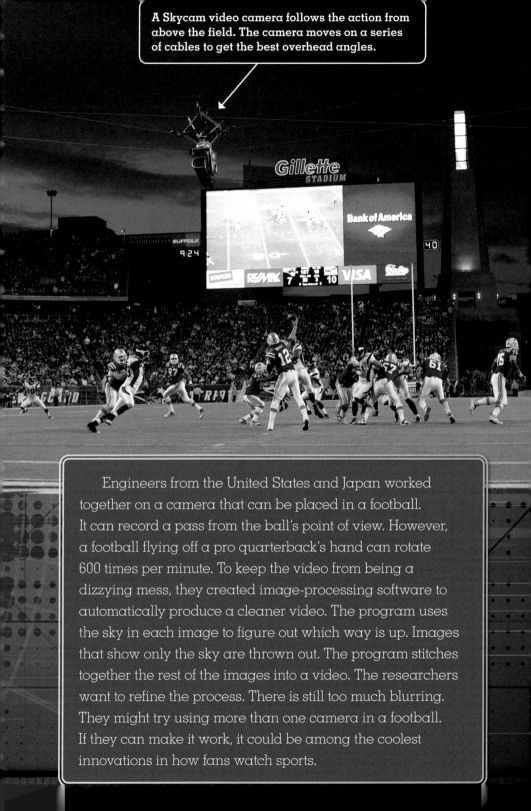

A Skycam video camera follows the action from above the field. The camera moves on a series of cables to get the best overhead angles.

Engineers from the United States and Japan worked together on a camera that can be placed in a football. It can record a pass from the ball's point of view. However, a football flying off a pro quarterback's hand can rotate 600 times per minute. To keep the video from being a dizzying mess, they created image-processing software to automatically produce a cleaner video. The program uses the sky in each image to figure out which way is up. Images that show only the sky are thrown out. The program stitches together the rest of the images into a video. The researchers want to refine the process. There is still too much blurring. They might try using more than one camera in a football. If they can make it work, it could be among the coolest innovations in how fans watch sports.

CHAPTER 1

Tools of the Trade

BALLS

FOOTBALLS

More engineering technology is in the works for footballs. In goal line stands, referees often can't see where the ball is, even with video replays. A sensor in the ball would help make an accurate call. A computer chip, along with thin cables placed along the sidelines and goal lines, could track the football's exact location. The referee would then know exactly where to spot the ball, whether it's a first down or if it crossed the goal line.

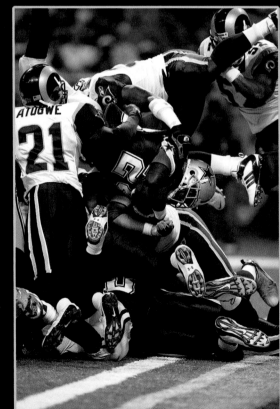

A pileup near the end zone can make it difficult for referees to tell if a player has scored a touchdown.

GOLF BALLS

A golf ball is made in layers. The golf ball's inner core is made of rubber or hard plastic. The core is surrounded by a soft outer core with a much harder plastic outside. A soft, thin polyurethane cover is the final layer.

Golf ball layers can be made in various ways to improve both distance and control. The hard inner core takes most of the energy from the swing and puts it into distance. The softer outer shell helps irons grip the surface and give the ball spin when it's needed.

Each dimple in a golf ball makes a tiny bubble of air above the ball as it sails toward the green. These little whirlpools of air make the air around the ball flow smoothly around it. The ball flies farther than if it had a smooth surface.

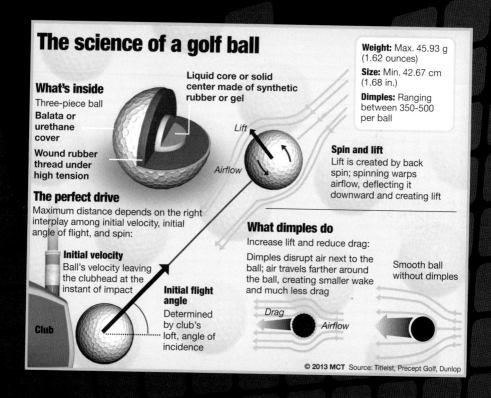

The science of a golf ball

Weight: Max. 45.93 g (1.62 ounces)
Size: Min. 42.67 cm (1.68 in.)
Dimples: Ranging between 350-500 per ball

What's inside
Three-piece ball
Balata or urethane cover
Wound rubber thread under high tension

Liquid core or solid center made of synthetic rubber or gel

Lift

Airflow

Spin and lift
Lift is created by back spin; spinning warps airflow, deflecting it downward and creating lift

The perfect drive
Maximum distance depends on the right interplay among initial velocity, initial angle of flight, and spin:

Initial velocity
Ball's velocity leaving the clubhead at the instant of impact

Initial flight angle
Determined by club's loft, angle of incidence

Club

What dimples do
Increase lift and reduce drag:
Dimples disrupt air next to the ball; air travels farther around the ball, creating smaller wake and much less drag

Smooth ball without dimples

Drag

Airflow

© 2013 MCT Source: Titleist, Precept Golf, Dunlop

FACT
Polyurethane is a **durable**, flexible plastic. It can be made to be hard, sticky, bouncy, stretchy, or squishy. It can also be made to resist heat and moisture.

durable—able to last a long time   **7**

TENNIS BALLS

Pro tennis players can smash the ball up to 150 miles (240 kilometers) per hour. When a tennis ball takes a beating like that, its shape might change throughout the match. Engineers use a machine to **compress** tennis balls to test them. The balls need to withstand being squashed repeatedly to be able to stand up to a pro tennis match.

A tennis ball changes shape as it hits a racket's strings.

BOWLING BALLS

Rolling a heavy plastic ball toward pins is a simple concept. But when bowlers are striving for perfection, they use balls with materials designed for their own styles.

The durable material in a bowling ball is mixed with various **resins**. The resin on the outside of the ball affects how well the ball grips the lane and hooks before it gets to the pins. The materials used on the outer shell can have tiny particles mixed in to help with the grip.

Engineers test various balls on a real lane to find out what materials work best. Accurate tests require a bowler with a perfect motion on every roll. People aren't perfect, so engineers built a robot to do the job. Every roll is measured with sensors placed along the lane. The ball's speed and path are saved in a computer. The engineers study the data from dozens of rolls to see if the ball performed as expected.

compress—to squeeze together into less space

resin—a semisolid substance made when oil and gas are refined; resin is used to make plastics

SOCCER BALLS

Adidas developed the familiar black and white soccer ball for the 1970 World Cup. The flat hexagons and pentagons were stitched together into a round shape. But the design caused a couple of problems. The stitching made the ball slightly less round, and the ball could change shape throughout the game.

Brazil's Michel Bastos lines up a kick against North Korea's Cha Jong Hyok during the 2010 World Cup.

For the 2006 World Cup, the familiar pattern was replaced by 14 curved panels bonded together with heat. This time the ball kept its round shape better during a match.

The Jabulani was designed for the 2010 World Cup. The new ball is made of eight curved panels. Adidas also added "aero grooves" to the outside of the ball. The grooves help players control the ball better and make the ball's flight more stable.

BASEBALLS

The design of baseballs used in the major leagues hasn't changed much in the last 100 years. A baseball has a cork and rubber sphere in the middle called the pill. The pill is a little smaller than a golf ball. Four layers of wool and cotton are wound tightly around the pill. The first—and thickest—layer is made of wool. Wool goes back to its original round shape quickly after being compressed by a slugger's hit. The outer layer is cowhide. The cowhide is carefully tested for thickness, strength, stretch, and resistance before being wrapped around the ball.

FACT
Until 1974 the outer surfaces of pro baseballs were made of horsehide. Major League Baseball switched to cowhide that year.

Bats, clubs, sticks, and rackets have gone through major changes in recent years. Engineers have developed creative ways to make them lighter and more powerful.

COMPOSITES

Engineers use composites in tennis rackets and golf clubs, as well as surfboards, arrows, and rowing oars. Composites are made of more than one material. Composites are usually a combination of glass or carbon fibers and liquid resin. When the resin hardens, the new composite has lighter weight, greater strength, and more power. Various combinations of carbon and resin can be used to make various types of composite materials.

Adam Scott

DESIGNING FOR POWER

Tennis rackets were once made of wood. The rackets tended to break, and they didn't help the player generate much power.

Composites allow manufacturers to distribute the racket's weight. The manufacturers might design a tennis racket with more weight toward the head, which increases the swing weight. Swing weight is how heavy a racket feels during a swing. Two rackets can weigh the same but have different swing weights. A higher swing weight leads to more power.

Engineers have also designed a racket that uses a spring lever to absorb the energy upon impact with the ball. The arm rocks back, creating a pocket within the strings. As the ball leaves the strings, the arm springs forward, releasing the stored energy and giving the ball more speed.

Roger Federer

GOLF CLUBS

A balance between a golfer's strength and a club's swing weight will help his or her game immensely. When it comes to golf clubs, most woods aren't made of wood anymore. Many are aluminum or steel. Some woods are made of titanium, which is a strong, lightweight metal. Titanium has a more consistent collision with the ball to give the golfer more control. Titanium clubs are also more durable than wood. However, titanium is expensive.

Golf swing analysis software helps golfers improve their game.

The official pro rules allow golf clubs to be made of any material. Engineers use computer-aided design programs to experiment with various weights and shapes of the club head. Golf club designers have made an important discovery. Placing more weight around the edges of the club head reduces how much the club twists if it hits the ball off center.

HOCKEY STICKS

A hockey slap shot is one of the fastest motions in sports. The design of hockey sticks, along with the player's shot technique, makes the puck fly across the ice. Most hockey sticks are made of graphite and composites. The stick flexes for a moment when it hits the ice behind the puck, which adds energy to the shot. The puck is in contact with the stick blade for only hundredths of a second, but the **force** on the puck is about 100 pounds (45 kilograms).

A hockey stick is designed to bend during a slap shot before straightening out again.

Miguel Cabrera

BASEBALL BATS

Swing weight is important with baseball bats too. More swing weight means more power. But bat speed has been found to be more important than swing weight. If the bat's swing weight is too high, it can slow the hitter's bat speed. If the player is consistently swinging late, the bat's swing weight might be too high. In that case the player should pick a bat with a lower swing weight or work on increasing his or her strength.

force—an act that changes the movement of an object

A hockey player takes a hard check into the boards. The jarring hit snaps his head to the side as it bounces off the glass. A linebacker makes a diving tackle. His head slams into the running back's shoulder pad. A softball player diving into home plate crashes into the catcher. The side of the runner's head hits the catcher's knee. In all of these plays, the player gets up right away because of well-designed helmets.

As good as current helmets are, engineers are working to improve them. They study the helmets' **elasticity**. An elastic material returns to its original shape after being stretched or expanded. If the material regains its shape too quickly, the impact energy doesn't spread out. The length of the impact needs to be increased for the helmet to absorb more of the energy.

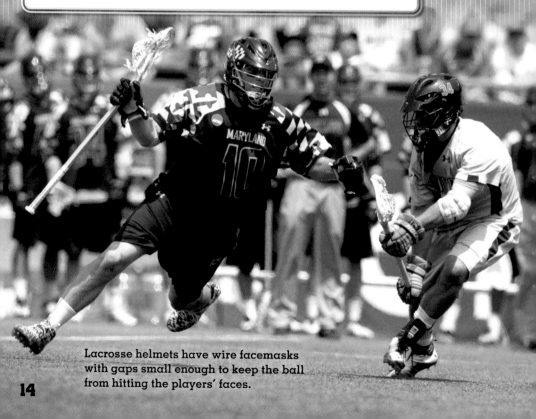

Lacrosse helmets have wire facemasks with gaps small enough to keep the ball from hitting the players' faces.

A regular football helmet is misshapen slightly in an impact. It regains its shape in a couple of milliseconds. The helmet is not absorbing much of the collision's energy. A better helmet would regain its shape in about half a second, allowing more time for energy to be absorbed. The helmet would be safer since more energy would be absorbed.

HOW IS A HELMET LIKE A RACETRACK?

An important part of protecting athletes is absorbing the energy of an impact. That's the idea behind what NASCAR has done at its racetracks. The track walls were once solid concrete. When a car crashed into it, the wall didn't budge. The result was a torn up car and possibly an injured driver—or worse.

A soft wall, known as a SAFER barrier, is now in place at all tracks where NASCAR races. A wall of hollow steel tubing with foam padding in front of it stands in front of the concrete. The barrier caves in at impact, absorbing the energy of the crash. The impact of a crash takes about 0.15 second longer than if the car hit concrete. The longer impact means the wall absorbs more of the energy.

SAFER stands for Steel and Foam Energy Reduction.

elasticity—the ability of a material to stretch or compress and return to its original size and shape

SHOES

Shoes can be designed to help a player's quickness and speed, as well as to help prevent injury. There's a lot of competition among companies that make athletic shoes. They continue to design new technology for this important piece of equipment.

RUNNING SHOES

Long-distance runners want the lightest shoes possible. One running shoe Nike designed weighs only 5.6 ounces (160 grams) for a size-9 shoe. It's made of lightweight yarn and other fabrics knitted into it to make it feel like a layer of skin. The exact materials are a secret, but we do know that it took engineers four years of research and testing to create the best mix.

Mike Trout

CLEATS

In baseball, football, and soccer, players need to be able to change direction quickly on grass or artificial turf. Metal or plastic studs allow their feet to grip the ground. Tennis players on a grass court also need to change direction quickly, accelerate in a short space, and do it without sliding. But cleats on their shoes would tear the court to shreds. Tennis shoes for grass courts are designed with rubbery pegs on the soles. They give the player grip without causing injury and without destroying the court.

ICE SKATES

Skates used for hockey are very different from those used for figure skating. The blades on hockey skates are usually shorter. They also have two edges on the bottom. The design helps players dig into the ice for quick turns and explosive starts.

Figure skaters need to be no less explosive in their movements. Figure skates are designed with a toe pick. This jagged edge at the front of the skate helps skaters grip the ice for jumps and spins.

SHOE TESTING

Testing shoes for the best performance can take some high-tech engineering. One test uses thousands of tiny pressure sensors. The sensors are hooked to a computer. They record how much pressure is applied in all parts of the inside of the shoe when someone runs, shuffles, and jumps. Every foot is different, so the results can show what type of shoe is perfect for an individual athlete.

Studies on running are used to test shoes, clothes, and even a person's running style.

REDUCING ANKLE SPRAINS

The solution to ankle sprains for basketball players was once high-tops or ankle braces. The idea was to prevent the ankle from rolling over during a hard stop or pivot. If the ankle remained locked in place, it wouldn't sprain, right? But ankle sprains still happened.

Research is now focused on better ways to keep the ankle safe without locking it in place. Some shoes help

prevent sprains by allowing only some ankle **ligaments** to move. The player still has some flexibility, but there is less movement in the ligaments that are most prone to spraining.

WHEELCHAIR DESIGN

Engineers have designed wheelchairs to be used in sports. In wheelchair rugby, for example, players can slam into each other with their chairs. The chairs have three large wheels and four small wheels. Rugby is a rough game, so the chair needs to be built to withstand the collisions.

Engineers focus on the chair's **center of gravity** to keep it upright. The center of gravity needs to be low to keep the chair from tipping over. Therefore, the seat is placed lower and the wheels are angled outward. The player is harder to tip over when more weight is lower in the chair.

For wheelchair racing, the chair only has three large wheels. The third wheel is in front and allows athletes to lean forward to be more aerodynamic with more force. The wheelchairs are made of composite materials, including a lightweight carbon fiber.

ligament—a band of tissue that connects or supports bones and joints

center of gravity—the point at which a person's mass is evenly distributed in all directions

EQUIPMENT TESTING

To build better equipment, engineers need to know about the forces acting on the equipment. They conduct tests to study how the equipment performs and how it can hold up against various types of use.

SNOWBOARDS

Engineers place strain gauges all over a snowboard to test how the board's shape changes when in use. The gauges measure the stretch of a snowboard. An **accelerometer** records vibrations to see how much the board shakes. Engineers use the data to figure out the best materials for a snowboard.

Engineers have also invented a snowboarding robot to test snowboards. Humans aren't very consistent, but a robot can do the same thing over and over to see how the board reacts. The robot has a set of air-powered **pistons** that pump up and down. The movements of the pistons simulate the moves a snowboarder makes.

Shaun White

accelerometer—a special device that measures the strength and length of forces created by an impact

piston—a solid cylinder or disk that moves up and down within a tube

Germany's Maria Riesch

SKIS

Skis are made of many materials, including plastic, metal, and polyurethane. Some skis are made of fiberglass—layers of glass fibers mixed with glue. Fiberglass is good at twisting and bending without breaking. Engineers can layer the fibers in various patterns to make them stronger and more flexible, without twisting too much.

SKI BOOTS

Ski boots used to be stiff and didn't allow much ankle movement. An inventor studied space suits and got an idea for a better ski boot. A system of tubes and wiring inside a space suit monitors pressure and temperature. If the tubes and wires become kinked, the suits can't keep the pressure and temperature at safe levels. The space suit's joints have ridges that allow a range of motion without kinking, like a flexible drinking straw.

Ski boots now use this space suit design. A skier's foot can move, but the boot keeps the ankle stable. Skiers have more control and a greater range of motion for their feet. The boot also makes it harder for skiers to hurt their ankles.

CHAPTER 2

The Field of Play

Sports engineers have focused a lot of their attention on making the field of play competitive, challenging, and safe. After all, that's where the action takes place. The engineers work on improving natural surfaces, but they also invent new kinds of surfaces to enhance the gameplay.

REAL OR ARTIFICIAL TURF? HOW ABOUT BOTH!

Many fans and athletes don't like artificial turf. But natural turf takes a lot of work to maintain. Scientists and engineers have developed ways to make natural turf better to play on while able to stand up to wear and weather. A mix of both turns out to be a good solution. A mixed field has millions of strands of plastic below the surface with 1 inch (2.5 centimeters) exposed on the top. Natural grass grows between the artificial fibers. This strong support structure for the grass keeps the field strong and firm and prevents sod from tearing off the surface.

LAMBEAU FIELD

Games can get cold late in the football season at Lambeau Field in Green Bay, Wisconsin. Engineers developed a way to keep the field from freezing in the frigid winter. A heating system under the field helps maintain the surface, even when grass is not growing. A system of plastic tubes lies about 1 foot (0.3 meter) under the surface. A liquid substance with antifreeze moves through the tubes and helps regulate the field's temperature. This technology is also used to keep some baseball fields warm in early spring so grass can begin growing.

Snow can be a problem for players at Lambeau Field, but the heating system under the ground keeps the surface in good condition.

THE ASTRODOME

When the Houston Astrodome opened in 1965, it was the world's first domed stadium. It was the stadium wonder of its time. The roof had skylights to allow sunlight to come in. It had natural turf at first. But players soon realized the skylights made fly balls hard to see. The skylights were painted over, which made using natural turf impossible. The solution: Astroturf. This plastic grass allowed indoor baseball and football. Reliant Stadium replaced the Astrodome, but the innovative design of the old dome inspired other modern stadiums.

The Astrodome

ON THE ICE

Winter sports need high-quality ice. The ice thickness has to be perfect. If it's too thick, the systems that keep the ice frozen have to work too hard. If it's too thin, skate blades can break through it.

Freezing salt water runs through pipes under the rink's floor. The cold fluid keeps the concrete under the ice below freezing. The best quality ice has to be built up in layers. Sprayers make several passes across the rink. Lines are painted in between the layers. The paint actually freezes onto the ice.

Monthly refrigeration costs reach thousands of dollars for an indoor ice rink. It can take 15,000 gallons (56,781 liters) of water to make ice for some rinks. Besides that, up to 150 gallons (568 liters) of water are needed for resurfacing during games or skating competitions.

On the other hand, artificial ice doesn't need any water. It's used most often in places where it's difficult to maintain a frozen surface. Artificial ice is made of pieces of plastic material. A slippery liquid is sprayed on the fake ice that allows skates to glide on it. However, some players say synthetic ice doesn't feel the same as real ice. It's slower, and they have to work a little harder to go fast. But it is a good surface for beginners to learn on.

Panels of artificial ice fit together like puzzle pieces.

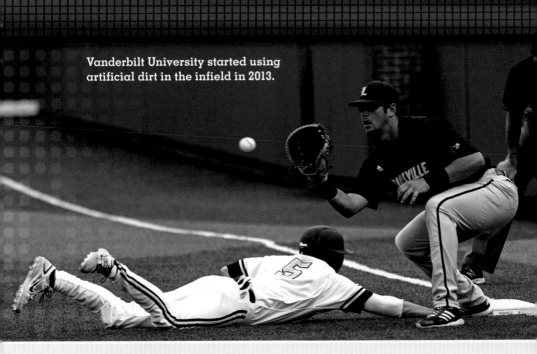

Vanderbilt University started using artificial dirt in the infield in 2013.

ARTIFICIAL DIRT

Another type of artificial surface has found its way into sports—fake dirt. In horse racing it is used to make the track more stable and cushiony, which reduces the chance of leg injuries for the horses. It also keeps the horses from kicking up dust.

Artificial dirt is easier to care for too. After a heavy rain, real dirt becomes sloppy and muddy. Artificial dirt dries quickly to make the surface ready for competition more quickly after a rain.

If artificial dirt works for horse racing, could it work for baseball or softball fields? Although people like to see dust fly when a player slides into base, some baseball and softball fields have begun using artificial dirt. The dirt is made of crushed lava rock, sand, and finely shredded plastic. These fields can be ready for play 30 minutes after a hard rain.

FACT
One company makes artificial dirt out of recycled athletic shoes. The shoes are shredded and mixed with sand to create a stable surface with good cushioning and traction.

players and fans.

SHATTERING THE BACKBOARD

Vicious dunks are an eye-popping part of basketball. During the 1960s and 1970s, the hoops weren't built to withstand the player's weight. Backboards were prone to shattering. As fun as it was for fans to watch, shattering backboards was not safe.

Today a strong device holds the rim to most backboards. If someone dunks a basketball and pulls on the rim, the device allows the rim to flex downward, taking pressure off the backboard. Hoops also include a stiff spring. The spring allows the rim to snap back into place after the player lets go.

GOLF COURSE DESIGN

Engineers strive to design challenging and unique golf courses. Elevation maps help engineers study the drainage of an area before building a course. They have to know where rainwater will flow and how it will affect the water traps. To avoid flooding in the water traps, dams or storm drain systems may be built.

FACT
Engineers use satellite imagery to see the terrain fairways will be built on.

RACETRACKS

On a flat racetrack, a race car going too fast on a turn will skid out of control. Banked turns keep the cars on the track and their speeds high. When the banking is steeper, the cars can go even faster.

The NASCAR tracks at Martinsville, Virginia, and Fontana, California, have almost the same degree of banking. Martinsville is banked 12 degrees on turns, and Fontana is banked 14 degrees. They should look about the same, right? The Fontana track actually appears to be much more banked than Martinsville. The different widths of the two tracks make Fontana appear much steeper. Fontana is 75 feet (23 meters) wide. Martinsville is only 55 feet (17 m) wide.

Martinsville Speedway

BOBSLED TRACK TESTING

Bobsled track designers walk a fine line between challenge and safety. Before a bobsled run is built, engineers test speeds by measuring the **friction** between the sled runners and the ice. That's tricky to do on an actual run, so they build **simulators**.

Engineers in Germany built a large drum that is 12 feet (3.7 m) wide and looks a little like a washing machine. The inside of the drum has a layer of ice. A machine presses runners to the ice to simulate the weight of the crew in the sled. The drum rotates to simulate actual bobsled speeds while the runners slide along the ice, up to 93 miles (150 km) per hour. With the data from the simulation, engineers can determine the maximum speeds a sled can reach at all parts of the track.

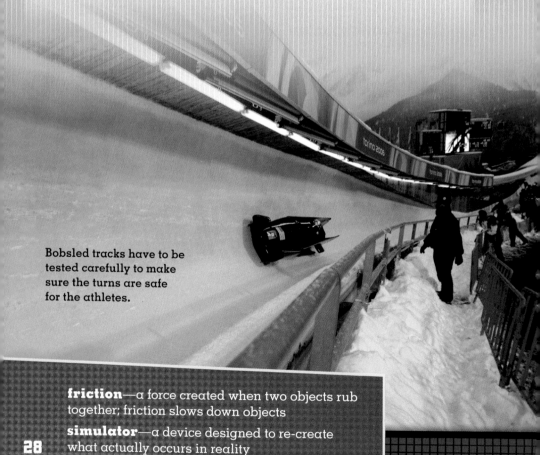

Bobsled tracks have to be tested carefully to make sure the turns are safe for the athletes.

friction—a force created when two objects rub together; friction slows down objects

simulator—a device designed to re-create what actually occurs in reality

A snowboarder goes upside down during a trick while practicing on a Snowflex half pipe.

SNOWFLEX

There isn't much snow in England, but that doesn't stop skiers. They used to rely on artificial surfaces that didn't feel much like real snow. The biggest problem was that the surface had to have the same properties as snow. Snow is slippery and allows you to speed down a slope. But it also has grip. When you cut an edge while skiing, the ski grabs the snow as you turn.

Inventors designed a composite material for skiing and snowboarding: Snowflex. Equipment rides on Snowflex just like on snow. The surface of Snowflex, though, makes it great for learning or experimenting with tricks more safely. A misting system keeps the surface slippery. The surface doesn't need to be groomed like real ski slopes do.

THE BEST IN
SPORTS VENUES

Stadiums are designed to give fans a great experience while watching their favorite teams. The Pittsburgh Pirates' stadium, for example, is said to have the best view for fans. The highest seat is just 88 feet (27 m) from the baseball field.

AT&T STADIUM

Dallas, Texas, is home to the world's largest column-free building: AT&T Stadium. The stadium cost more than $1 billion and can seat 100,000 fans. Two huge arches, each nearly 300 feet (91 m) high and 1,290 feet (393 m) long, hover above the field. The Statue of Liberty would be able to fit inside the stadium!

It takes an engineering feat just to move the enormous glass doors at each end zone. They are 180 feet (55 m) wide and 120 feet (37 m) tall. Each of the five moveable panels weighs 58 tons (53 metric tons). Wheels at the bottom of the panels move along rails on the floor. Two 10-horsepower motors drive the wheels. With the doors open, the building has the feel of an open-air stadium.

The stadium also has the second-largest video screen of any stadium. The huge video board weighs 600 tons (544 metric tons) and is suspended 90 feet (27 m) above the field. Engineers built a steel structure $71\frac{1}{2}$ feet (22 m) tall to support the massive display.

SAFECO FIELD IN SEATTLE

Safeco Field's retractable roof acts like an umbrella. It moves into place during Seattle's frequent rain showers. The design lets in natural light so it still feels like an outdoor game.

FACT

Reliant Stadium in Houston, Texas, built two new video screens in 2013. Each screen is 14,549 square feet (1,352 square meters), surpassing the size of the giant screen in AT&T Stadium.

UNIVERSITY OF PHOENIX STADIUM

Home of the Arizona Cardinals, the University of Phoenix Stadium has some remarkable engineering features. Its retractable roof is the first ever built on a slope. The roof panels move on wheels that run along curved rails. For this to work, the rails have to be almost perfectly **parallel**—within $\frac{1}{16}$ of an inch (1.6 millimeters).

The roof panels are made of a fabric called Bird-Air that is a combination of fiberglass and Teflon. The material is durable, lightweight, and strong. It can support 17,000 pounds (7,711 kg) per square foot, but it's as thin as fabric. The material is **translucent**, so sunlight can come in, which creates an open feeling even when the roof is closed.

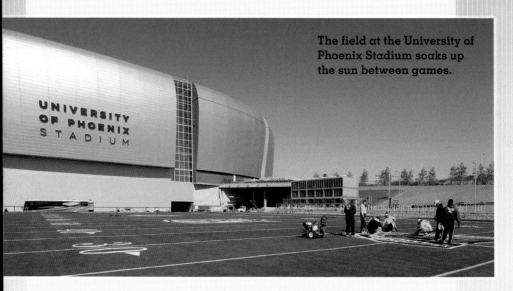

The field at the University of Phoenix Stadium soaks up the sun between games.

The stadium also has something that no other stadium in the country has—a retractable field. The field rolls in and out of the stadium on steel rails. The grass soaks up the Arizona sun when there isn't a game.

parallel—an equal distance apart at all points

translucent—partially see-through; allowing some rays of light to pass through

Rexall Tennis Centre

REXALL TENNIS CENTRE

Because of the smaller playing surface of tennis courts, tennis stadiums are also smaller. But that's good for fans—every fan is close to the action. That's especially the case at Rexall Tennis Centre in Toronto, Canada. The seating area is shaped like a paraboloid. The lower-level seating sections are flatter, and the second level has steeper rows. All seats have clear views of the entire court.

Wembley Stadium

WEMBLEY STADIUM

Wembley Stadium in London, England, has a unique look. A 436-foot- (133-meter-) tall arch supports a retractable roof. At 1,033 feet (315 m) long, the arch is the world's longest single span roof structure. There are no support columns to obstruct fans' views.

Tension in the spokes of a bicycle wheel pull the wheel together and allow it to withstand hard landings. The energy from the impact is spread out among all of the spokes. That design was the inspiration for how Wembley's arch can hold so much weight. Wires coming out of the arch work like giant spokes. The wires are huge tension cables that pull the roof up toward the arch. The cables in turn support the arch. The arch above Wembley Stadium is visible for 13 miles (21 km) across London.

FACT
An arch is one of the strongest support structures ever designed. It moves the force of the weight it's supporting to the legs.

THE SAPPORO DOME

The Sapporo Dome in Sapporo, Japan, looks like a futuristic vacuum cleaner. But its genius engineering allows it to be a baseball stadium and a soccer stadium using two separate fields.

The soccer field can be rolled outside during a baseball game. When it's time to play soccer, the soccer field is brought back inside and rotated 90 degrees. The seating in center field folds up, and the outfield wall slides away to make room for the soccer field to be moved in and out.

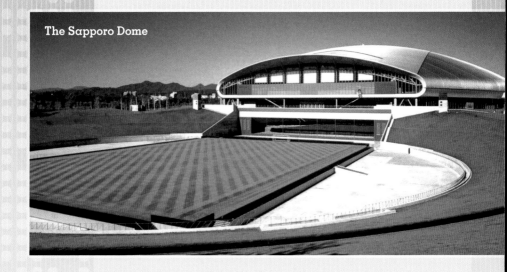

The Sapporo Dome

Unlike the football field in Phoenix that rolls along rails, the soccer field in Sapporo floats in and out of the field. Air pressure raises the 8.3-ton (7.5-metric-ton) field 3 inches (7.6 cm) off the ground. The structure also moves on 34 wheels, taking about two hours to move inside or outside.

CHAPTER 3

Innovations in Sports Design and Engineering

Sports engineers have the power to radically change a sport or create a new sport. There is no end to their creativity. Innovations add excitement and safety to the world of sports.

WHERE THE URETHANE MEETS THE ROAD

Early skateboards had metal or clay wheels. The wheels made it difficult to control the board, and the rough ride was bone-jarring. Skateboarding suddenly became popular in the 1970s when board designers started using urethane to make the wheels.

Urethane grips the pavement, but the wheels will slide if the rider pushes hard enough. Urethane wheels provide a smooth ride and great control. They make it possible for skaters to do tricks, jumps, and cut turns while maintaining control.

The grip of a skateboard's wheels helps the rider perform aerial tricks.

FREEBORD

An engineer named Steen Strand wanted to find a way to make skateboarding feel more like snowboarding. Then snowboarders could ride on the street when there was no snow on the ground. The Freebord can do the same carving and sliding that snowboarders do on snow.

Strand made an extra wide truck for the board. The truck provided more stability for carving wide turns. He then added a center wheel on each truck that can turn all the way around.

A snowboard can ride sideways, but a skateboard can't. On a Freebord, the outer wheels simulate the edges of a snowboard. The rider moves his or her weight to the edge to carve a turn. The wider wheel base on the Freebord makes it possible.

Freebords allow more flexibility and movement than a regular skateboard.

BIOMEDICAL ENGINEERING

Biomedical engineers study how body tissues heal. They use magnetic resonance imaging (MRI) to see muscle tissue up close. An MRI uses a super-strong magnet to see inside the body. Biomedical engineers can see when the muscles fire and how much force they use. They can then figure out which muscle groups do the most work. They can also monitor how an athlete is recovering after a muscle injury.

Sports trainers use medical software and equipment to assess injuries.

POUNDING THE PAVEMENT

Runners are in great physical shape, but their knees take a pounding. Knees absorb a lot of energy with every step. Biomedical engineers can use computer simulations to help runners change their running style to help reduce injury. They can study how runners' muscles are used at various speeds and if a runner uses longer or shorter strides.

For one experiment, 40 reflective markers were placed on runners. They ran on treadmills. Eight cameras recorded their motion. Models were made of the runners' leg muscles and skeletal structures. The study concluded that if the runners took slightly shorter steps while running, they could reduce their risk for injury or soreness in their knees.

Runners compete during the men's marathon at the 2012 Olympics.

WHAT TO WEAR

MONITORING AN ATHLETE'S BODY TEMPERATURE

Keeping athletes safe is especially important in hot weather. Late summer football practices and games can cause players' body temperatures to become dangerously high. If they don't cool down in time, they can get heat exhaustion or heat stroke, which can be fatal.

NASA helped develop a thermometer pill that can be swallowed. The device sends astronauts' core body temperatures to a computer. It works great for athletes playing or practicing in hot weather.

Tracking player temperatures

Some NFL teams already use a system that features vitamin-sized "radio pills" to monitor players' core body temperatures during practice.

The pill

- Outer silicone coat
- Communication coils
- Temperature sensing crystal
- Battery

How it works

- Player swallows "pill" the night before practice or early the next morning
- Pill transmits up to 300 ft. (90 m) to handheld personal digital assistant (shown below)
- Pills last 24-36 hours before passing out of the human body

Personal digital assistant

- PDA displays data in real time for each player
- System has high temperature alert feature
- System monitors up to 99 players at one time

© 2013 MCT
Source: HQ-Inc.
Graphic: St. Paul Pioneer Press

FACT

The thermometer pill is also used by firefighters as they battle fires and by divers in cold water.

Apolo Ohno

NOT A DRAG

Speed skaters and downhill skiers race at incredible speeds. The enemy of speed is **drag**. Engineers use materials to make clothing that is stronger and lighter. The clothing is designed to operate like a golf ball. A rough surface allows the athlete to glide through the air better whether sliding down a luge hill, flying off a ski jump, or flying along the ice in speed skating.

CLEARING UP THE FOG

During a 1966 mission, astronaut Eugene Cernan was in orbit wearing a jet-propelled backpack outside the spacecraft. He was performing tests in preparation for astronauts landing on the moon. His space walk had to be cut short because his goggles kept fogging up. Since the body is naturally warm and moist, **condensation** settles on the slightly cooler smooth goggle surface, making it difficult to see. Seeing is pretty important both in space and in many sports, such as downhill skiing. NASA scientists designed a compound made from liquid detergent, water, and fire-resistant oil. The chemical has been used to keep ski goggles and deep-sea diving masks clear.

drag—the force created when air strikes a moving object; drag slows down moving objects

condensation—changing from a gas to a liquid or solid

41

LIKE THE ANIMALS

To study the quickest and strongest athletes, engineers simply look at nature. They study the way animals move to create new design and engineering ideas. A gecko's feet, for example, can hold its weight on smooth surfaces. But how can we **mimic** a gecko's feet to help us make amazing football catches?

Engineers studied the gripping power of a gecko's feet to make equipment for athletes.

Geckos have millions of hairlike strands on their feet. Each strand splits into hundreds of tiny tips that help them stick to surfaces. Engineers are trying to find a way to use what geckos do to make nonskid shoes and sticky gloves for wide receivers.

Wearing a sharkskin swimsuit, Tunisia's Oussama Mellouli won the gold medal for the 1500-meter freestyle event during the 2008 Olympics.

SHARKSKIN SWIMSUIT

Engineers created a sharkskin swimsuit in the early 2000s. It was designed to mimic the tiny ridges and bumps on a shark's skin. The ridges and bumps reduce drag in the water and help a shark move quickly and smoothly. They helped swimmers in the same way. During 2008 and 2009, swimmers broke at least 130 world records while wearing the suits.

The polyurethane material in some of the suits was made in panels. The panels were heated and fused together instead of stitched so there were no seams. Seams would create more drag for the swimmer. The panels in some suits also trapped little pockets of air, which gave swimmers more **buoyancy**.

While the suits were an engineering success, they seemed to give swimmers an unfair advantage. The polyurethane panels and high-tech suits were banned in 2010.

mimic—to copy

buoyancy—the tendency of an object to float or rise when submerged in a fluid

NANOTUBES

Scientists are discovering more materials to enhance equipment and athletes' performances. They developed something better than the carbon fibers used in composites: carbon nanotubes. They are even lighter and stronger than composites made of carbon fibers, but they can be expensive.

A carbon nanotube is a tiny cylinder of carbon atoms. Imagine a sheet of paper made of carbon atoms but only as thick as one atom. Each atom is shaped like a hexagon, a very strong structure. Roll that sheet into a tube, and the result is a carbon nanotube. The tiny nanotube is hundreds of times stronger than steel and one-sixth as heavy.

Nanotubes can be used to coat bicycle parts, skis, baseball bats, and other sports equipment to make them lighter and stronger. The technology continues to advance, and engineers keep working on ways to find more uses for nanotubes.

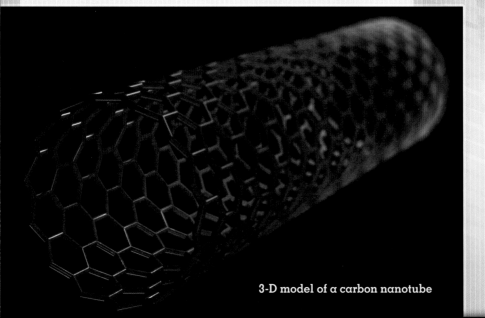

3-D model of a carbon nanotube

COMPUTER MODELING

Ansys is a company that has designed software that can simulate almost anything. Computer programs predict what will happen to materials under certain conditions without needing to test the materials in real life. Computers do the work much more quickly.

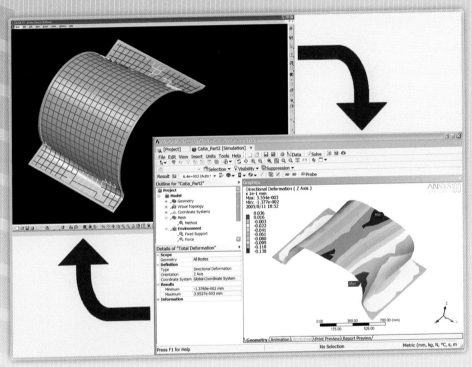

Ansys' Fibersim computer program provides data about how composite fibers react during testing.

Engineers can invent a new kind of tennis racket, for example, without having to wreck hundreds of them in the process. A computer can simulate millions of designs hitting a ball countless times to see how the material will wear over time. Engineers can test rackets, bats, or any other sports equipment.

GLOSSARY

accelerometer—a special device that measures the strength and length of forces created by an impact

buoyancy—the tendency of an object to float or rise when submerged in a fluid

center of gravity—the point at which a person's mass is evenly distributed in all directions

compress—to squeeze together into less space

condensation—changing from a gas to a liquid or solid

drag—the force created when air strikes a moving object; drag slows down moving objects

durable—able to last a long time

elasticity—the ability of a material to stretch or compress and return to its original size and shape

force—an act that changes the movement of an object

friction—a force created when two objects rub together; friction slows down objects

ligament—a band of tissue that connects or supports bones and joints

mimic—to copy

parallel—an equal distance apart at all points

piston—a solid cylinder or disk that moves up and down within a tube

resin—a semisolid substance made when oil and gas are refined; resin is used to make plastics

simulator—a device designed to re-create what actually occurs in reality

translucent—partially see-through; allowing some rays of light to pass through

READ MORE

Adamson, Thomas K. *The Technology of Baseball.* Sports Illustrated Kids. North Mankato, Minn.: Capstone Press, 2013.

Creighton, Jayne. *Sports.* New York: Weigl Publishers, 2010.

Perritano, John. *Sports Science.* New York: Marshall Cavendish Benchmark, 2011.

Ross, Stewart. *Sports Technology.* Mankato, Minn.: Smart Apple Media, 2012.

INTERNET SITES

FactHound offers a safe, fun way to find Internet sites related to this book. All of the sites on FactHound have been researched by our staff.

Here's all you do:

Visit *www.facthound.com*

Type in this code: 9781476541556

Super-cool stuff!

Check out projects, games and lots more at
www.capstonekids.com

INDEX